1,000,000 Books

are available to read at

www.ForgottenBooks.com

Read online
Download PDF
Purchase in print

ISBN 978-1-332-01823-9
PIBN 10269569

English
Français
Deutsche
Italiano
Español
Português

www.forgottenbooks.com

Mythology Photography **Fiction**
Fishing Christianity **Art** Cooking
Essays Buddhism Freemasonry
Medicine **Biology** Music **Ancient
Egypt** Evolution Carpentry Physics
Dance Geology **Mathematics** Fitness
Shakespeare **Folklore** Yoga Marketing
Confidence Immortality Biographies
Poetry **Psychology** Witchcraft
Electronics Chemistry History **Law**
Accounting **Philosophy** Anthropology
Alchemy Drama Quantum Mechanics
Atheism Sexual Health **Ancient History**
Entrepreneurship Languages Sport
Paleontology Needlework Islam
Metaphysics Investment Archaeology
Parenting Statistics Criminology
Motivational

INSTRUCTIONS

FOR THE

AINING OF PLATOONS
R OFFENSIVE ACTION

1917

▽

Part   I—Organization and Tactics
Part II—Training
Part III—General Remarks
Appendixes

WAR DEPARTMENT,
Document No. 613.
Office of The Adjutant General.

WAR DEPARTMENT,
WASHINGTON, *June 14, 1917.*
The following Instructions for the Training of Platoons for Offensive Action are published for the information of all concerned.

[2622804 A. G. O.]

BY ORDER OF THE SECRETARY OF WAR:

TASKER H. BLISS,
Major General, Acting Chief of Staff.

OFFICIAL ::

H. P. McCAIN,
The Adjutant General.

3

INTRODUCTION.

The instructions herewith are in extenso of those contained in Section IV, paragraph 5 of S. S. 135, Instructions for the Training of Divisions for Offensive Action, and must be read in conjunction therewith.

In the last-mentioned document it is laid down, as a result of recent experience, that the platoon is the unit in the assault. The organization of a platoon has been decided in G. H. Q. letter O. B./1919, dated February 7, 1917. The guiding principles of this organization are that the platoon shall consist of a combination of all the weapons with which the Infantry are now armed, and that specialist commanders for Infantry are undesirable.

In O. B./1919/T, dated February 14, 1917 (S. S. 144), a normal formation for the attack, of which the platoon is the unit, has been laid down. The adoption of a normal formation for the attack has been necessitated partly by the shortness of the time which is available for training, and partly by the lack of experience among subordinate commanders.

This pamphlet has been drawn up with a view to assisting platoon commanders in training and fighting their platoons. It is not possible to lay down a correct line of action for all situations which may arise on the battle field, but it is hoped that a careful study of the instructions herein contained may assist subordinate commanders to act correctly in any situation.

The terms "trench-to-trench attack" and "attack in open warfare" are used in this pamphlet to differentiate from an instructional point of view between the methodical attack of highly organized defenses and such attacks as may occur at a later period of an offensive after the main system of the enemy's defenses has been penetrated.

It can not be too thoroughly recognized that although it may be necessary to slightly vary the preparations and form of assembly for the attack in these two sets of circumstances, the actual tactics to be employed will usually be identical.

5

CONTENTS.

INSTRUCTIONS FOR THE TRAINING OF PLATOONS FOR OFFENSIVE ACTION, 1917.

PART I.—ORGANIZATION AND TACTICS.

1. ORGANIZATION OF A PLATOON.

The platoon is the smallest unit in the field which comprises all the weapons with which the Infantry soldier is armed. It has a minimum strength, exclusive of its headquarters, of 28 O. R. and a maximum of 44 O. R. If the strength falls below the minimum, the platoon ceases to be workable, and the necessary numbers will be obtained by the temporary almalgamation of companies, platoons, or sections under battalion arrangements.

Taking an average strength in the sections of 36 O. R., a suitable organization would be as follows:

	Total O. R.
Headquarters—1 officer and 4 O. R.	4
1 section bombers—1 N. C. O. and 8 O. R. (includes 2 bayonet men and 2 throwers)	9
1 section Lewis gunners—1 N. C. O. and 8 O. R. (includes Nos. 1 and 2)	9
1 section riflemen—1 N. C. O. and 8 O. R. (picked shots, scouts, picked bayonet fighters)	9
1 section rifle bombers—1 N. C. O. and 8 O. R. (includes 4 bomb firers)	9
Total	36

Every N. C. O and man should carry a rifle and fix his bayonet for the assault, except Nos. 1 and 2 of Lewis gun and rifle bombers, if using a cup attachment.

2. PARADE.

The platoon should parade in line, sections at two paces internal, or in column of sections; commanders should be two paces in front of their sections.

3. Ammunitiom, Bombs, etc., and how Carried.

In each section enough ammunition and bombs can be carried for immediate requirements.

In the trench-to-trench attack every man (except bombers, signalers, scouts, runners, and Lewis gunners who carry 50 rounds) carries at least 120 rounds S. A. A. and 2 or more bombs.

The Lewis gun section carries 30 drums (a good method is 2 haversacks joined with slings or braces, 1 on chest—2 drums; 1 on back—3 drums).

In bombing sections each thrower carries 5 bombs, and the remainder 10 or more each. •

Every man in a rifle bomb section can carry at least 6 rifle bombs (a good method is a haversack carried on the back with six or more holes punched in the bottom to take the stick, canvas being attached to the haversack in shape of a bag to protect the sticks).

Flares must be distributed throughout sections.

Two P. bombs should be carried by each "mopper up" in addition to other descriptions.

Any further requirements in S.A.A. bombs, etc., must be met by carrying parties from other companies specially detailed.

In open warfare the number of bombs to be carried in the section of bombers and rifle bombs in rifle bomb sections may be regulated according to the objectives to be attacked.

4. Characteristics and Uses of the Various Weapons.

(a) The rifle and bayonet, being the most efficient offensive weapons of the soldier, are for assault, for repelling attack, or for obtaining superiority of fire. Every N.C.O. and man in the platoon must be proficient in their use.

(b) The bomb is the second weapon of every N.C.O. and man, and is used either for dislodging the enemy from behind cover or killing him below ground.

(c) The rifle bomb is the "howitzer" of the infantry and used to dislodge the enemy from behind cover and to obtain superiority of fire by driving him underground.

(d) The Lewis gun is the weapon of opportunity. Its chief uses are to kill the enemy above ground and to obtain superiority of fire. Its mobility and the small target it and its team present render it peculiarly suitable for working round an enemy's flank or for guarding one's own flank.

5. The Normal Formations for Platoons and Companies in the Attack.

A. TRENCH-TO-TRENCH ATTACK.

The platoon.—Appendix I shows a platoon in 1st and 2nd waves. Appendix II shows a platoon in artillery formation of sections. These can move in fours, file or single file, according to the ground and other factors. Platoon H.Q. should move with that column best situated for purposes of command; this will usually be the rear section.

The company.—Appendix III shows the normal formation of a company in two waves, in which the formation of the platoon remains the same.

B. OPEN WARFARE (APPENDIX IV).

The formation may conveniently be the same as the above when deployment first takes place. The first wave becomes the firing line, the second wave the supports.

" Moppers up " will not usually be required.

6. Working and Carrying Parties.

Working and carrying parties should be detailed by complete sections under their leaders, irrespective of the weapon with which they are armed. They should never be found by detailing a certain number of men from the platoon.

A platoon acting as a carrying party should move in file, the sergeant at the head with the guide, the platoon commander bringing up the rear. The pace at the head should be slow and section commanders must pass down word if they can not keep up.

When a platoon is detailed for a working party its commander, and no one else, is responsible for the quality and quantity of work performed; he can not take too much interest in this matter.

7. Tactics of a Platoon in Attack.

In either a trench-to-trench attack or in open warfare these resolve themselves in the majority of cases into the method of attack of tactical points.

A tactical point may be described as a locality, the possession of which is of first importance locally to either side. It may take the form of any of the following: A "strong point," the junction of a communication trench, a cross roads, a bank, a hedge, a house, or other locality of limited dimensions.

The tactics to be employed may be summarized as follows:

(i) Push on to the objective at all costs and get in with the bayonet.

(ii) If held up, obtain superiority of fire and envelop one or both flanks.

(iii) If reinforcing another platoon which is held up, help to obtain superiority of fire and envelop a flank.

(iv) Cooperate with platoons on either flank.

For purposes of instruction these may be considered under: A. Trench-to-trench attack; B. Attack in open warfare.

A. TRENCH-TO-TRENCH ATTACK (APPENDIXES VIII AND IX).

In regard to—

(i) No further comment is necessary, other than to lay stress on the point that waves must go direct above ground to their objective.

(ii) The action of the various sections and commanders should be as follows:

The section of riflemen should, without halting, gain a position on a flank from which to attack both with fire and with the bayonet.

The section of bombers should, without halting, gain a position on a.flank and attack under cover of the bombardment of rifle bombs.

The section of rifle bombers should open a hurricane bombardment on the point of resistance from the nearest cover available.

The section of Lewis gunners should in the first instance open traversing fire on the point of resistance from the nearest cover available. At a later stage it may be desirable to work round a flank.

Section commanders control and lead their sections, keeping touch with the platoon commander.

The platoon commander controls and directs the sections and sends back information to the company commander.

(iii) One of the most important factors in the action of a platoon reinforcing another is that of its commander. He should make himself acquainted with the situation before he commits his platoon to any line of action. This is called the personal reconnaissance of the commander.

(iv) The means to be employed in cooperation depend so greatly upon the circumstances at the moment that it is impossible to lay down a definite line of action to adopt. Cooperation means help. If a neighboring platoon is held up, one of the surest ways of helping it is to push on. Touch must always be maintained; this can be effected by means of a patrol of two men, as well as by signal.

B. ATTACK IN OPEN WARFARE (APPENDIXES X TO XIII).

The line of action described above will usually be found suitable. Owing to the more extended field of action, however, the use of scouts and the personal reconnaissance of the platoon commander become of increased importance.

Great opportunities will also occur for mutual support from rifles or Lewis guns for the movement of neighboring sections and platoons.

8. THE TACTICS OF THE PLATOON IN DEFENSE.

In both trench and open warfare the action to be taken in the defense is practically the same, namely, to hold ground by occupying mutually supporting tactical points, so situated as to be screened from artillery fire, and to obtain—

(i) Observation.

(ii) Field of fire for all rifles.

(iii) Enfilade fire for the Lewis gun.

For these purposes the analogy between trench and open warfare is not far to seek. For instance, in occupying a captured position—

" Consolidation " in trench warfare corresponds to the occupation of an " outpost position " in open warfare.

" Observation posts " in trench warfare corresponds to "sentry groups " in open warfare.

" Strong points " in trench warfare corresponds to " picquets " in open warfare.

In both cases the necessity for visiting and reconnoitering patrols is equally important.

9. General Rules as to Tactics.

In regard to all tactical situations on the battlefield, the old principles are applicable both to trench warfare and to open warfare, and should become a second nature or subconscious habit. They may be summarized as follows:

(i) Aim at surprise, i. e., see without being seen. Do not let bayonets show over the parapet, and take care the assembly is not given away by perceptible movement.

(ii) Reconnoiter before movement; that is to say, work by "bounds," making ground good with scouts before advancing to it.

(iii) Protection. Never remain halted on the field of battle without a lookout. Sentries must be posted, no matter what troops are supposed to be in front.

(iv) The flanks. (a) Guard your own flanks and keep touch with neighboring units; (b) try and get the enemy's flank. For example: (a) In trench warfare booming and Lewis gun sections guard the outer flank and liaison is kept with neighboring units; in open warfare scouts must always be employed on an outer flank, one section, usually the Lewis gun section, must be told off to act in that direction if necessary, and touch must always be kept with troops on either flank. (b) Employ enveloping tactics.

(v) Send information back to your company commander. Negative information is as important as positive. You can not expect assistance from your superiors or from the artillery unless you tell them where you are and how you are situated.

(vi) Hold what you gain. Never withdraw from a position without being ordered to do so. If where you are is unhealthy and appears untenable owing to casualties, any attempt at withdrawal—anyhow in daylight—will end in increased casualties. Therefore, stay where you are and send back information.

PART II.—TRAINING.

1. To obtain uniformity of ideas and tactics it is necessary for the method to be followed in training platoons to be laid down on broad lines.

2. The requirements to be attained are:

(*a*) The offensive spirit. All ranks must be taught that their aim and object is to come to close quarters with the enemy as quickly as possible so as to be able to use the bayonet. This must become a second nature.

(*b*) Initiative. The matter of control by even company leaders on the battle field is now so difficult that the smaller formations—i. e., platoon and section commanders—must be trained to take the necessary action on their own initiative, without waiting for orders.

(*c*) Confidence in weapons, necessitating a high standard of skill at arms.

(*d*) Cooperation of weapons is essential on the battle field, and is the corollary of (*c*).

(*e*) Discipline is most necessary at all times, and particularly on the battle field.

(*f*) Morale must be heightened by every possible means; confidence in leaders and weapons goes a long way toward it.

(*g*) Esprit de corps. True soldierly spirit must be built up in sections and platoons. Each section should consider itself the best section in the platoon, and the platoon the best in the battalion.

3. The method of attaining these requirements is as follows:

(i) The platoon commander should divide the time allotted to him for training into two periods, the first being devoted to individual and section training and the second to collective or platoon training and tactical exercises.

(ii) Training should be progressive, beginning with section drill without arms, saluting, etc., working up to battle formations and tactical exercises.

(iii) A refresher course every evening for section leaders, in which the next day's work should be gone through, is essential: if they are shaky in it, they should practice it then and there.

(iv) A high standard of skill at arms can only be produced by both the platoon commander and platoon sergeant being proficient in the use of and able to impart instruction in all the weapons with which the platoon is armed.

(v) Soldierly spirit in the platoon and sections is obtained by encouraging section leaders to take a pride in their sections and in their work. The formation adopted in falling in on platoon parades tends to bring this about. Section leaders should inspect their sections before the platoon commander inspects the platoon, and they should report them correct or otherwise. At evening entertainments and lectures regimental history and accounts of skill at arms and feats of daring on the battle field should be given prominence.

All ranks must be trained in the following:

(vi) Steady drill and ceremonial are necessary to inculcate discipline, of which cleanliness, smartness, and steadiness are the bedrock.

(vii) Bayonet fighting produces lust for blood; much may be accomplished in billets in wet weather, as well as out of doors on fine days.

(viii) Bomb throwing and duties of moppers-up require practice and careful study. Moppers-up should work in pairs under their own commander. They drop into their objective and work laterally outward. They kill any enemy met with in the trenches and guard the entrances to dugouts and side trenches. They must not penetrate down into the dugouts before the platoon for which they are mopping up arrives.

(ix) Musketry: Too much stress can not be laid on practicing the standard tests laid down in musketry regulations. These can be practiced in billets on wet days just as well as out of doors. Tripods and aim correctors are easily improvised. Good bolt manipulation, produced chiefly by the application of the standard tests in the barrack room on wet days, kept the enemy out of our trenches at the beginning of the war, when such luxuries as wire entanglements were not forthcoming. Ranges also are easily improvised.

(x) Physical fitness: Route marching, physical training, and recreational training, such as football, paper chases, etc. These latter are best carried out on Wednesday and Saturday afternoons, which, if training is progressing satisfactorily, may be half holidays.

(xi) Fire discipline.

(xii) Wiring.

(xiii) Field works and filing on tasks: The placing of frames for mined dugouts may suitably be included in platoon training.

(xiv) Work in the field: Tactical exercises in which the use of ground and choice of cover in both trench and open warfare must receive close attention are most necessary. An intelligent use of ground frequently enables forward movement to be made without loss. In choice of cover, as a general rule, anything marked on a map or very well defined should, if possible, be avoided to obviate casualties from shell fire. Such exercises can be carried out, as a rule, within a few hundred yards of billets; it is seldom necessary to waste time by going too far afield, except when route marching and march discipline is being practiced. Schemes should comprise the attack of tactical points in trench and open warfare, the action of a platoon, as vanguard to an advance guard, an outpost picket, etc. The platoon sergeant and section commanders can be usefully trained by this means when the men are otherwise employed; it enhances their powers of initiative.

(xv) Gas drill, including bombing, bayonet fighting, and musketry with masks or box respirators on.

Sections must be exercised in their particular weapon:

(xvi) The bombing section in bombing attack.

(xvii) The rifle bombing section in quickly forming a rifle bomb bombardment or barrage.

(xviii) The Lewis gun section in coming into action and opening fire quickly.

(xix) The rifle section. The training of this section is very important. Each man should be a marksman, first-class with bayonet and bomb, and a scout, in addition to being either a Lewis gunner or rifle bomber.

Training in certain other subjects is necessary for certain individuals:

(xx) Section commanders. Fire control and description of targets, map reading, observation, and information. Salient points in writing messages. Simple tactical exercises.

(xxi) Scouts and snipers. Map reading, observation, information, and salient points in writing messages and use of appliances. Each section should produce a pair.

(xxii) Runners and dispatch carriers. How to find an individual and how to deliver a message.

Certain training must be practiced by night as' well as day, namely:

(xxiii) Bayonet fighting, bomb throwing, Lewis gun firing, musketry, wiring, running and dispatch carrying, and tactical exercises.

(xxiv) Live ammunition. No form of instruction with arms can be considered complete until it has been carried out with live ammunition under conditions as nearly as possible approaching those which would pertain on the battle field.

(xxv) Competitions. Each form of instruction should be made the subject of a competition, from saluting and clean turnout up to musketry, accuracy of rifle bombs, scouting, sniping, etc., etc. Prizes are seldom necessary for such competitions, if the result is published in battalion orders.

(xxvi) Thoroughness. As regards dress and arrangements generally, no part of the training should be perfunctory ; that is to say, nothing should be left to the imagination ; work must always be based on the actual ground and situation as they exist. The turnout should always be in fighting order, with haversacks properly packed and with the full complement of arms and ammunition which would be carried in battle.

PART III.—GENERAL REMARKS.

A platoon commander will have gone a long way toward having a well-trained platoon if he has gained the confidence of his noncommissioned officers and men and has established a high soldierly spirit in all ranks.

The confidence of his men can be gained by—

(*a*) Being the best man at arms in the platoon, or trying to be so.

(*b*) Being quick to act, taking real command on all occasions, issuing clear orders, and not forgetting to see them carried out.

(*c*) Example, being himself well turned out, punctual, and cheery even under adverse circumstances.

(*d*) Enforcing strict discipline at all times. This must be a willing discipline, not a sulky one. Be just, but do not be soft—men despise softness.

(*e*) Recognizing a good effort, even if it is not really successful. A word of praise when deserved produces better results than incessant faultfinding.

(*f*) Looking after his men's comfort before his own and never sparing himself.

(*g*) Demanding a high standard on all occasions, and never resting content with what he takes over, be it on the battle field or in billets. Everything is capable of improvement from information on the battle field down to latrines and washing places in billets.

(*h*) Being bloodthirsty, and forever thinking how to kill the enemy and helping his men to do so.

The platoon commander should be the proudest man in the Army. He is commander of the unit in the attack. He is the only commander who can know intimately the character and capabilities of each man under him. He can, if he is so disposed, establish an esprit de platoon which will be hard to equal in any other formation.

APPENDIX I.

The Platoon, Taking an Average Strength of 36 and H.Q. 4— Formation for Trench-to-Trench Attack.

(Showing 2 platoons in 2 waves, with the right the outer flank.)

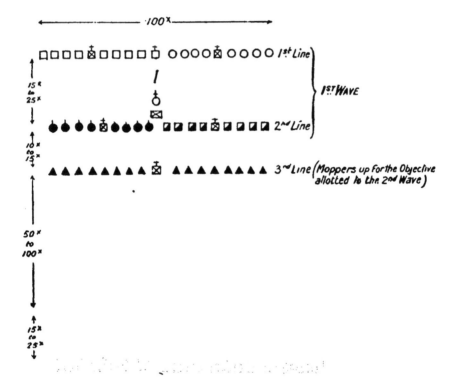

Key :—

Ŏ Platoon Commander.   □ Rifleman.   ● Rifle Bomber.
Ů Platoon Sergeant.   ▨ Lewis Gunner.   ▲ Mopper Up.
⊠ Section Commander.   O Bomber.   ⊠ Platoon H.Q.

NOTES.

Two platoons are depicted, showing the different positions of leaders in first and second waves.

The platoon is the unit in the assault, moves in one wave of two lines, and has one definite objective.

Every man is a rifleman and a bomber, and in the assault, with the exception of the No. 1 and No. 2 of the Lewis gun, fixes his bayonet. Men in rifle sections must be trained either to the Lewis gun or rifle bomb.

Bombing and Lewis gun sections are on the outer flank of platoons.

In assembly, the distance between lines and waves may conveniently
be reduced to lessen the danger of rear waves being caught in enemy
barrage, the distance being increased when the advance takes place.

"Moppers up" follow the second line of a wave and precede the
unit for which they are to mop up. If the numbers are large, they
must be found from a different company or battalion. Small numbers
are preferably found from the unit for which they are to mop up.
They must carry a distinctive badge and have their own commander.

G.S.

O.B. No. 1919/T

APPENDIX II.

The Platoon in Artillery Formation with the Right the Outer Flank.

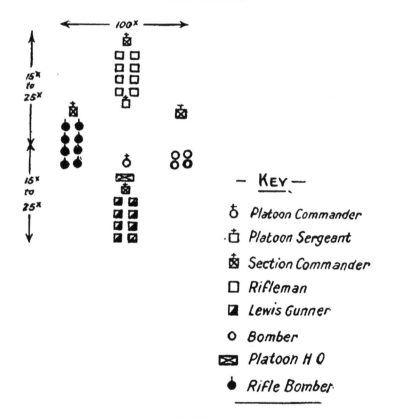

NOTES.

Sections move in fours, file, or single file, according to the ground
and other factors of the case.

Platoon H.Q. moves with that column best suited for purposes of
command.

APPENDIX III.

The Company, Taking 4 Average Strength **Platoons of 36** O.R. and Coy. H.Q. 14.—**Formation for Trench-to-Trench** Attack.

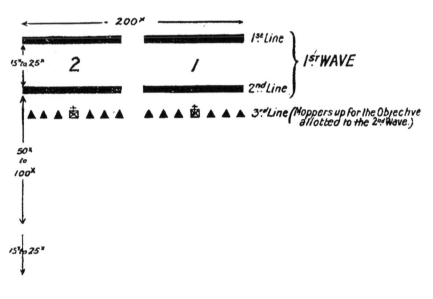

Key :— ⚛ Coy. Commander.　　▬ Platoon (in 2 lines).

      ✉ Coy. H.Q.　　▬

                           ▲ Moppers up.

NOTES.

The company moves in two waves, has two objectives, and is distributed in depth.

"Moppers up" follow the second line of a wave and precede the unit for which they are to mop up. If the numbers are large they must be found from a different company or battalion. Small numbers are preferably found from the unit for which they are to mop up. They must carry a distinctive badge and have their own commander.

G.S.
O.B.   No.   1919/T

APPENDIX IV.

The Platoon, Taking an Average Strength of 36 and H.Q. 4.— Formation for Attack in Open Warfare.

(Showing two platoons in two lines, with the right the outer flanks.)

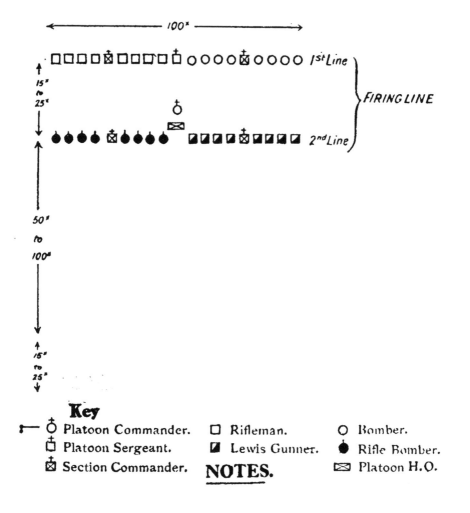

Key

Ȯ Platoon Commander.	☐ Rifleman.	◯ Bomber.
Ů Platoon Sergeant.	◪ Lewis Gunner.	● Rifle Bomber.
⊠ Section Commander.	**NOTES.**	⊠ Platoon H.O.

NOTES.

Two platoons are depicted showing the different positions of leaders in firing line and supports.

The platoon is the unit, has one definite objective, and can move in two lines, as above, or form one line as circumstances dictate. Two lines are most easily obtained from artillery formation.

Every man is a rifleman and a bomber, and in the assault, with the exception of the No. 1 of Lewis gun, fixes his bayonet. Men in rifle sections must be trained either to the Lewis gun or rifle bomb.

Bombing and Lewis-gun sections are on the outer flank of platoons.

The number of bombs and rifle grenades to be carried will be decided by the nature of the objective distance to be traversed and other considerations.

G.S.
O.B. No. 1919/T

APPENDIX V.

Suggested daily program during summér months:

FIRST PERIOD.

Before breakfast: Section drill.

After breakfast: One hour each section in its own weapons, the rifle sections being allotted half to the Lewis gun section and half to the rifle bomb section. One hour the whole platoon bomb throwing. One hour physical training and bayonet fighting.

Finish the morning with ceremonial; that is to say, form up and march past the platoon or company commander on the way to dinner.

After dinner: Communicating drill and control of fire drill. Musketry on the range alternately by sections. Recreation at 4 p. m. Noncommissioned officers refreshed in the next day's work at 6.30 p. m.

APPENDIX VI.

SECOND PERIOD.

Before breakfast: Platoon drill.

After breakfast: Half hour whole platoon bomb throwing. One hour instruction in wiring, digging, and filing on tasks; scouts and snipers—information, map reading, and message writing; runners and dispatch carriers; moppers up. One hour physical and bayonet training. Last half hour fire control and fire discipline. Ceremonial on the way to dinner.

After dinner: Simple tactical schemes. Recreation at 4 p. m. Noncommissioned officers refreshed in the next day's work at 6.30 p. m. Simple tactical schemes.

NOTE TO SUGGESTED PROGRAM.

For examples of exercises in the field both in trench-to-trench attack and in open warfare see Appendixes VII to XIII.

If training is progressing satisfactorily, half-holidays should be allowed on Wednesdays and Saturdays.

Men who prove themselves efficient should be excused certain parades. Individual keenness is easily promoted and easily rewarded.

During winter months work should not begin till after breakfasts, e. g., at 8.30 a. m. The half-holidays are of greater importance than during the summer, because on other days there is not sufficient light after 4 p. m. for games.

Smoking concerts and lectures should be given on Wednesday and Saturday evenings.

APPENDIX VII.

EXAMPLES OF USEFUL EXERCISES IN OPEN WARFARE.

1. *Advance or flank-guard schemes.*—The platoon finding the advance parties is held up by a tactical point, necessitating a fight.   (See Appendixes X and XII.)

Points to be watched:

(i) The use of ground and scouts.

(ii) The correct use of weapons.

(iii) The plan should be that of enveloping tactics.

2. *Outpost schemes.*—This should involve the placing of each individual on the actual ground.   For instance, sentry groups, the sentry over the picket, reliefs for visiting and reconnoitering patrols, deciding what points are to be held, and how they are to be held in event of attack, the placing of the Lewis gun.

3. A tactical point is encountered with a machine gun.   Tactics of the supporting platoon.   Particular attention should be paid to the personal reconnaissance of the commander to the use of ground and weapons, and to the plan, which should be of the nature of enveloping tactics.   (See Appendixes VIII, IX, X, and XII.)

4. *Village fighting.*—In this the Lewis gun can be employed to keep down the enemy's rifle fire, while bayonet men and bombers bound down the right-hand side of the street, clearing house by house.   It is always better, if possible, to enter a house from the back rather than the front.

5. *Wood fighting.*—A line of skirmishers who fire while advancing (v. par. 8 of S. S. 135, Instructions for the Training of Divisions for Offensive Action), followed by sections in small columns, has been found a convenient formation.   Much attention to keeping direction is necessary.

APPENDIX VIII.

Trench-to-Trench Attack—Platoon in First Wave Meeting a Point of Resistance.

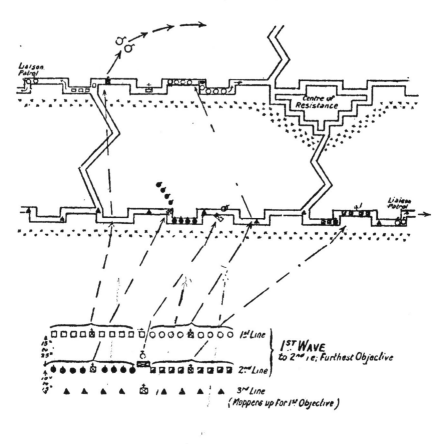

Key :— Ò Platoon Commander.   ▣ Lewis Gunner.   ▲ Mopper Up.
⬚ Platoon Sergeant.   ⫼ Lewis Gun in Action.   ⊠ Platoon H.Q.
⊠ Section Commander.   O Bomber.   δ Scout.
⬜ Rifleman.   ● Rifle Bomber.

NOTE.

The position of the commander.

The rifle bombs and Lewis gun fire and rifle fire are obtaining superiority over the enemey's fire.

The bombers and riflemen have gone straight above ground to their objective, where they are turning the flank of the center of resistance.

The use of scouts and liaison patrols.

The "moppers up" are guarding the entrances to dugouts and communication trenches.

APPENDIX IX.

Trench-to-Trench Attack—Platoon in Second Wave Meeting a Point of Resistance.

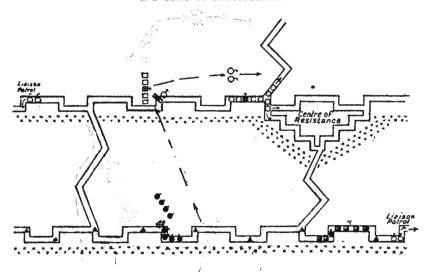

Key ⊢─ ○ Platoon Commander.　　🂠 Lewis Gunner.　　▲ Mopper Up.

　　　⟆ Platoon Sergeant.　　✟ Lewis Gun in Action.　　⊠ Platoon H.Q.

　　　⊗ Section Commander.　　○ Bomber.　　ᗆ Scout.

　　　☐ Rifleman.　　　　　　　◆ Rifle Bomber.

NOTE.

The commander of the second wave gets in touch with the situation on reaching his objective through the commander of his moppers up and the commander of the first wave. He then decides to help the first wave, the commander of which goes on to his own objective.

Note, especially in the action of the various sections, the attack above ground.

Attack in Open Warfare—Correct Method of Action of a Platoon in Firing Line, Meeting a Point of Resistance.

Key :—

ᐤ Platoon Commander

ᐁ Platoon Sergeant.

⚃ Section Commander

☐ Rifleman

◪ Lewis Gunner.

⊹ Lewis Gun in Action.

○ Bomber.

● Rifle Bomber.

✉ Platoon H.Q.

ᐤ Scout.

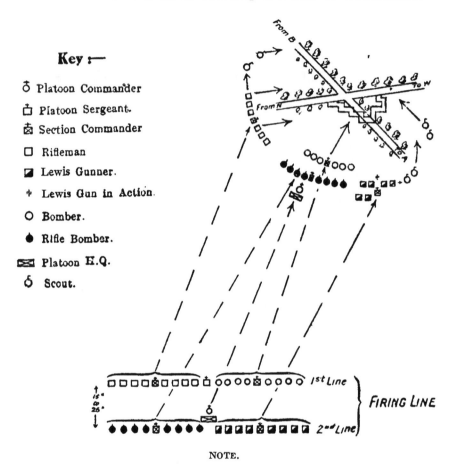

NOTE.

Correct use of scouts. Sections are under the hands of their commanders. A firing line has been built up, rifle, bombs, Lewis gun tire, and rifle fire are being used to obtain superiority over enemy fire. A flank is being turned.

APPENDIX XI.

Attack in Open Warfare—Incorrect Method of a Platoon in Firing Line, Meeting a Point of Resistance.

Key :—

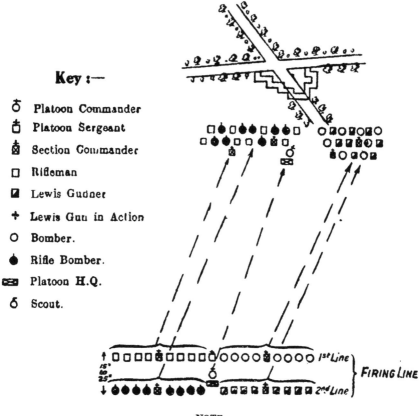

ᴓ Platoon Commander

ᴒ Platoon Sergeant

ᴕ Section Commander

▢ Rifleman

◪ Lewis Gunner

✝ Lewis Gun in Action

○ Bomber.

◕ Rifle Bomber.

▭ Platoon H.Q.

δ Scout.

1st Line

2nd Line

FIRING LINE

NOTE.

No scouts are employed.   Sections are mixed up and not under the hands of their commanders.   No firing line has been built up.   No attempt at enveloping tactics is being made.

APPENDIX XII.

Open Warfare—Correct Method of Action of a Platoon in Support.

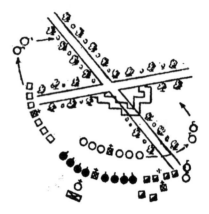

Key :—

♂	Platoon Commander.
⌷	Platoon Sergeant.
⊠	Section Commander.
☐	Rifleman.
◪	Lewis Gunner.
⫲	Lewis Gun in Action.
O	Bomber.
⊠	Platoon H.Q.
♂	Scout.
●	Rifle Bomber.

◻ ◻◻◻◉◻◻◻◻   ◖◦◗◦◗

NOTE.

The platoon commander is seen making his personal reconnaissance some hundred yards ahead, with the platoon waiting under cover under platoon sergeant. On result of this reconnaissance he can act on either flank, dependent on the ground and the situation.

APPENDIX XIII.

Open Warfare—Incorrect Method of Action of a Platoon in Support.

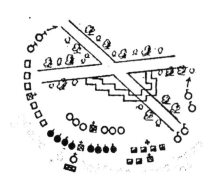

Key :—

Ỏ Platoon Commander.

Ḃ Platoon Sergeant,

⊠ Section Commander.

☐ Rifleman.

◪ Lewis Gunner.

✦ Lewis Gun in Action.

O Bomber.

♠ Rifle Bomber,

▨ Platoon H.Q.

ᗶ Scout.

NOTE.

The platoon commander of the supports is shown as having led his platoon right up to the platoon already engaged, where it arrives in confusion. He has made no personal reconnaissance and is committed to one flank only. This line of action could only be adopted where good cover exists immediately in rear of platoon engaged, in which case even, the platoon commander should have gone ahead and finished his personal reconnaissance by the time his platoon arrives.

O

WS - #0079 - 050221 - C0 - 229/152/2 - PB - 9781332018239